THE TED HEATH BUNKSIDE BOOK

Compiled by
NORMAN URE

LESLIE FREWIN OF LONDON

90p
Net (UK only)

Acknowledgements

Camera Press
Central Press Photos

Cover design : Frances O'Regan and Andrew Turvey
Cover design © Leslie Frewin Publishers Limited, 1971

(Thinks) *Good grief – not Barbara Castle in hot pants?*   Hi, Babs darling . . .

George Brown sings
Frank Sinatra at the Finsbury
Park Empire? You've just
got to be joking.

. . . and we guarantee folks, that one wash in our new wonder powder with the powerful blue 'C' ingredient, will remove everything from those grease stains on hubby's overalls to Harold Wilson's dirty habits.

Yes, that's it! I'll cash all my savings stamps first thing in the morning on my way to the betting shop and put the lot on Harold to win the next one by a landslide.

For goodness sake, dear,
take off that ridiculous hat and
start pumping the organ.
I'm on in 5 minutes.

Forgetting the sales for a moment —
how would you girls like to crew for me?

Madam, that's rude – but I like it!

What fun! I've never been on a protest march before.

Our Harold
Who art a heathen
Horrid be thy name . . .

Honest love —
I won't devalue it,
I only want a lick.

... now for Lot 206 — 1 lb of New Zealand butter.
Who'll offer me 75p?

Put your glasses on, Alec, I'm over here.

Ahoy there, Ma!
Your breast stroke's coming along fine.

Don't overdo it, Ted —
it's his mum you've got to
impress . . .

Don't worry, Reggie.
Tomorrow was yesterday
and now it's today.

What's he uptight about? Calling a spade a spade
has always stood me in good stead in the past.

You clumsy idiot, that
bottle of Krug cost me
six quid.

I hope I've managed to take your minds off all your problems so that you can
all concentrate on mine.

Then we have Sir Alec Douglas-Home, to name but four.

At a pinch, I suppose we could give her an extra
fiver a week – provided Philip is prepared to
tighten his belt a bit.

Really, messieurs,
I don't think Lord Longford
would approve of *that*.

One of the first things we've got to do, Alec,
is nationalise Private Eye.

It sounds a *lovely* idea, very tempting—
but I think I'll just sit here some
and watch you do *your* thing.

. . . and now I'd like you all
to turn to page ten of Mary
Wilson's Book of Poems,
and say after me . . .

Come on, Alec,
don't be sulky – think about
your popularity ratings.

It's all very nice having
the whole party behind me,
but if no one turns up
to listen . . .

I really can't decide between
the one with the teeth
or the one with the paunch . . .

Look here, Mabel – one more crack about Commonwealth sugar lumps and *you'll* do the washing-up.

I suppose we'd better go and pick up Philip and play this ruddy game of polo he keeps on about.

I agree with you Georges – what's £100 millions between friends?

Really, Harold – how can you expect me to let you take the solo in 'Nymphs and Shepherds' with that beastly pipe stuck in your mouth?

Of course I'm interested in Women's Lib –
but when do I get to meet Ann Summers?

Heavens above, Eamonn!
Not 'This Is Your Life'.

Do you really think the
blond rinse is an
improvement?

ust one more thing, Georges –
hen *will* Geoffrey and I be able to
eet the other Five?

Okay Mak, call off your strong-arm boys –
I'll come quietly.

Listen to that applause, Tony.
They love me,
don't they just *love* me?

Now, just once more for
Uncle Teddy—'E.E.C. stands for
EDWARD'S EVERYBODY'S
COMRADE...'

For the last time you
dumbheads – the arms we are
selling to South Africa are
not going to be used in
Dr. Barnard's transplant
programme.

This should be enough for the scullery curtains,
but if there's any over you can measure me up
for another pair of pyjama trousers.

Everybody's taking these French lessons
too seriously. I call a 'cabinet' meeting
and find six of my ministers squatting in
the private loo.

I'm sure that if I could get it to balance on the end of my nose, I'd get more laughs.

must say, Sir Alec, things have improved
ince I last travelled by London Transport.

I keep telling you, Robert, the Angry Brigade *can't* get you here.
The whole place is swarming with plainclothes men.

It's funny really, Willi –
now that we've got your
lot on our side the French
are agin us.

I'm single, good-looking, sophisticated,
with bags of the old savoir faire . . .
I suppose I *have* got everything when you think about it.

Now, just a moment, Robin — Ted's quite right you know —
that four-letter word isn't obscene *now*.

And finally, I would like to say to all my friends in Europe
that this is positively –

        Einde – (For all of you in Belgium)
        Fin – (For all of you in France)
        Het Einde – (For all of you in the Netherlands)
        La Fine – (For all of you in Italy)
        Fin – (For all of you in Luxembourg who speak French!)
        Ende – (For all of you in West Germany)
        THE END – (*Especially*, for all of you in Great Britain)

Publisher's Note

All royalties earned from this publication will be used by the author to set up a Trust Fund to build a public convenience at Chalk Farm, within easy reach of The Roundhouse. He hopes, eventually, to build a chain of these artistic monuments all over Europe. So please tell your friends to buy a copy of this book if they are interested in backing this worthy cause.